MW00477729

# Love Yourself First

# Love Yourself First

How to Heal from Toxic People, Create Healthy Relationships
& Become a Confident Woman

## Krystle Laughter

Fortre Publishing Co.

**Love Yourself First:** How to Heal from Toxic People, Create Healthy Relationships & Become a Confident Woman

© 2020 by Krystle Laughter

Published by Fortre Publishing Co.
Tacoma,WA 98409

Printed in the United States of America

All right reserved. No part of this publication may be reproduced, stored in a retrieval system, or transmitted in any form or by any means-electronic, digital, photocopy, recording, or any other- except for brief quotations in printed reviews, without the prior written permission of the author.

All Scripture quotations, unless otherwise stated, are taken from the New King James Version. Copyright © 1982 by Thomas Nelson, Inc. Used by permission. All rights reserved.

Scripture quotations marked CSB have been taken from the Christian Standard Bible®, Copyright © 2017 by Holman Bible Publishers. Used by permission. Christian Standard Bible, and CSB® are federally registered trademarks of Holman Bible Publishers.

Scripture quotations marked BSB are from The Holy Bible, Berean Study Bible. Copyright ©2016, 2018 by Bible Hub. Used by Permission. All Rights Reserved Worldwide.

Scripture quotations marked (CEV) are from the Contemporary English Version Copyright © 1991, 1992, 1995 by American Bible Society. Used by Permission.

*Cover & Interior Design by Krystle Laughter*

**ISBN 978-1-7346951-0-6**

# Table of Contents

**Introduction**............................................................ix

**1 How Did You Learn Love?**.........................13

    Pieces of Me (Part1)...................................17

    Why Not Love Yourself First?.....................20

    Make Yourself Happy...................................21

    History Repeats Itself.................................22

    Chapter 1 Review.......................................25

**2 Loving the Girl in the Mirror**....................27

    Pieces of Me (Part 2)..................................31

    Getting Real with Yourself?.........................34

    Do You Know You?......................................35

    How to Gain Self-Love................................35

    The Power of Words....................................37

    Chapter 2 Review.......................................41

**3 Becoming a Confident Woman**..................43

    Pieces of Me (Part 3)..................................47

    The Shame & Blame Mindset.......................53

    The Learning & Growth Mindset...................55

    Loving the Skin You're In............................57

    Chapter 3 Review.......................................61

**4 Creating Healthy Relationships**................................63

    Pieces of Me (Part 4)......................................67

    Believe What They Show You.....................70

    What You Allow Will Continue................71

    Let Them Lose You.......................................72

    Picky on Purpose...........................................74

    Love is on the Other Side of Fear................77

    Chapter 4 Review..........................................81

**5 Do You Lack Standards?**..............................83

    Pieces of Me (Part 5)......................................87

    What's it Costing You?.................................93

    Letting Go of the Past...................................95

    Face Your Fears.............................................98

    Birthing Boundaries....................................100

    Chapter 5 Review........................................103

**6 Girl, Go Get Your Healing**.........................105

    Pieces of Me (Part 6)....................................107

    The 3 "A's" of Healing................................113

    Discovering Your Worth.............................118

    Self-Love Everyday.....................................119

    Worth the Wait............................................122

    Chapter 6 Review........................................125

**Self-Love Affirmations**...............................127

**The 10 "I's of Self-Love**............................131

**Hello Today (Poem)**....................................135

**Resources**....................................................139

**About the Author**........................................141

*If you don't learn how to love yourself first, someone will offer you less than you deserve and you'll accept it.*

# Introduction

I've struggled with insecurity my whole life. I was always in awe of those who were confident, outspoken, and could easily stand up for themselves. Inwardly I wished I was bold and witty enough to be the class clown. As a child, I can remember being in school and being too shy to raise my hand to use the bathroom. I know it sounds silly, but that's just how shy I was.

I hated being called on to read aloud, even though I was a strong reader. I longed for attention, but in public it was painfully uncomfortable. It didn't help that I couldn't pronounce my R's right; I would use the W sound instead. When people would ask me my name it would come out, Kwistol instead of Krystle.

Reflecting back, I can see that I didn't speak up because I was afraid that others wouldn't like me. I feared rejection. It was easier to blend in with the crowd; being myself seemed like too much of a risk.

As a result, I was often forgotten and misunderstood. I still had friends, but I only let my guard down around those closest to me. I can still remember an elementary school dance. I wore a beautiful dark green dress and my mom had just done my hair. I was feeling like a princess. I watched everyone dancing and having a good time. I longed to dance, but every time I mustered up enough courage to get on the floor, something within would hold me back. My mom kept encouraging me to just go dance.

The boy I secretly had a crush on even asked me for a dance, and I bashfully declined. Minutes turned into hours and the dance was over. Till this day, I wish I could go back and cut it up. I would be the first one on and the last one off that dance floor. I wish I could have overcome my fear and insecurity to do what I really wanted to do... just dance.

As an adult, my insecurity led me down a dark road of toxic, regret-filled relationships. How did I keep winding up with people that didn't value me? How could I not see what others easily observed right away? Deep down inside, I was still that same little girl longing to be loved and accepted, never really feeling good enough. Now, I realize that I didn't know how to love myself.

No one ever told me I was worthy and valuable, so I never felt secure in my identity.

I didn't know that I had the power to love and accept myself because I had already been accepted by God.

It's sad as I think about the little girl longing to be enough. If I could go back in time, I would tell her how funny, creative, intelligent, and beautiful she really is. I would tell her to laugh, sing out loud, crack a joke, and never, ever stop dancing. Since I can't go back and tell her these things, I will tell you: Stop searching! Stop looking!

All of the love and acceptance you've ever needed is inside of you, placed there by God the moment you were created! You are enough. You are deserving. You are worthy. You are loved.

*I will praise You, for I am fearfully and wonderfully made; Marvelous are Your works, And that my soul knows very well.*

**-Psalm 139:14**

# How Did You Learn Love?

I

*If you don't learn how to love yourself first, you'll let people give you their worst while you give them your best.*

Who was your first example of love? For most of us, it was our parents. It's easy to underestimate the power of first impressions, reaching adulthood without ever stopping to think about how our experiences have shaped our view of life and love. What you witnessed and experienced growing up in regard to love has shaped your concept of love, your ability to love, and to be loved.

No matter what your upbringing was, it is vital that you take the time to reflect back on how you saw love being played out in the lives of those you love. For a lot of us, we saw love modeled in unhealthy ways.

If you witnessed abuse, you may believe that accepting toxic behaviors is a requirement to loving someone. Holding others accountable for their behavior may be challenging for you, because as a child you felt powerless to do anything, so you just learned to cope with inappropriate behaviors. A lot of women are in abusive relationships today as a result of the abuse they saw growing up.

I grew up as the youngest of six children in a single parent home. During that time, I witnessed my mother go through several toxic relationships. So, subconsciously you could say, one of the first lessons I learned about love was that unhealthy relationships were normal. I love my mother and I appreciate everything she did for me and my siblings. I applaud her strength. I know she did her best and I will always be truly grateful for her.

As I've said, my first introduction to love was very unhealthy. I witnessed women close to me date men who struggled with chemical dependency, mental health issues such as depression, and other toxic behaviors. A few of those relationships were physically abusive, which the police had to be called.

As I reflect back on the things I witnessed in those relationships, I recognize that they had more impact on me than I realized. I was a quiet child and I internalized a lot. I knew that I wanted better for myself when I got older. I knew that the way I saw relationships played out in the lives of those around me wasn't the way it was supposed to be.

I wouldn't be like them, I thought to myself. I was smarter than that. I would be different, I vowed to myself. I wouldn't allow men to mistreat me. I would choose men who loved me and knew how to treat me. I was better than that.

# Pieces of Me

Part I

Despite all my efforts to avoid the abuse I witnessed growing up, my first adult relationship was very unhealthy. It was with a very toxic man who wouldn't know love if Jesus came down and slapped him in the face. He was an older so-called "Christian". I was young, naive, and inexperienced. I'm sure he saw me coming from a mile away. He was nice at first, but the thought of a relationship with him repulsed me. I know it sounds terrible, but I must be honest. I told him that I didn't see him that way, but that didn't seem to deter him. One day as we were having breakfast at Denny's, he said that God told him that I was his wife.

I was more intrigued than anything else. I guess I continued to hang around him out of boredom and curiosity. Eventually and with much resistance on my part, he began to grow on me. I was awestruck by his knowledge of the Bible and how intelligent he appeared to be. His house contained hundreds of books that he had read. He was different than any man I have ever met. Eventually, we began dating and I got pregnant. The abuse followed immediately after that.

As I look back on that relationship, one of the mistakes I made was in believing that because he was older, he would appreciate me more than someone my own age. Sadly, this couldn't be farther from the truth. The first time he ever hit me was at a bus stop in broad daylight. He slapped me in the mouth like a parent would to a disobedient child. I think I was too shocked to really respond. I couldn't believe that it had happened. He later told me he did it because I had said something smart to him.

His agenda of gaining full control over my life happened quickly. He began by ostracizing me from my family after making up a story about how they unjustly cursed him out. I cut them off, only to find out years later that it was him that did the cursing. He had planned this all along. That's the only way he could get away with what was coming next.

Over the course of our three year relationship, we married and had two children. My children and I suffered physical, mental, and emotional abuse at his hands. I did my best to keep a smile on my face knowing the unspoken rules: never let anyone get too close, don't look in the direction of another man, and keep my mouth shut.

Despite my best efforts, he constantly belittled me; making me ask for food, refusing to let me breastfeed, forbidding me from taking the kids to the park, making me catch the bus pregnant, while he drove the family car. He wouldn't even allow me access to my own bank card, which held a whole five dollars. All the money I got from school was taken into his possession and spent as he saw fit. I was a prisoner without bars.

**To be Continued...**

# Why Not Love Yourself First?

As I have matured, I have come to understand that self-love is a necessity, because it is the foundation for which all of our love is based. If your foundation is broken, then the way you love others will be unhealthy and out of balance. You will give too much to others and expect little in return. You will be so happy to have someone to love that you won't stop to ask yourself if they deserve it. Self-love is vital because it teaches you to set standards and expectations of what you're willing to accept from other people and even yourself. Self-love is a foundational part of discovering your identity.

To some people self-love can seem selfish, but live long enough and you'll find that constantly meeting the needs of others is draining. When you make a habit of always putting other people's needs before your own, you will find that you have little or no time to do the things that you enjoy. This can be hard for mothers and caregivers. When you make time for yourself, you will be a better mother, friend, and person in general because your needs will have been met.

When you don't have self-love, you'll allow people to mishandle you and give you less than you deserve. On the flip side, self-love allows you to assess people and situations quickly.

It eliminates feelings of guilt from wanting more and knowing you deserve better. Self-love protects you from settling for less, because you know that you are worthy of everything you want and need. When you learn to love yourself first, it will be easier to let go of people and things that no longer serve you. Yes, it may hurt at first, but as you release negativity you will notice an improvement in your quality of life. So sis, learn to love yourself first. I promise you'll only lose those who never deserved you in the first place.

## Make Yourself Happy

Like me, some of us get into life and death situations because we are desperate for love and we think the only way to get it is from another person. The greatest source of love is from God. God is love! We only know what true love is because God showed us what love was through his son Jesus on the cross. Here is the definition of love given to us by God in the Bible:

*Love is patient, love is kind. It does not envy, it does not boast, it is not proud. It is not rude, it is not self-seeking, it is not easily angered, it keeps no account of wrongs. Love takes no pleasure in evil, but rejoices in the truth.*
*-1 Corinthians 13:4-6 (BSB)*

I don't think anyone would object to being loved like that, the problem is we never consider that we need to love ourselves like this. So much emphasis is placed on falling in love, getting married, and living happily ever after that most of us fail to realize that the majority of people don't know how to love themselves, much less another person. How many people looking for love have stopped to consider that the key to finding love is to love themselves first? Unfortunately, it took me thirty-four years to finally discover this truth. It's better late than never.

## History Repeats Itself

Now that I have children of my own, I realize that they learn best by example and not by instruction. If I want them to be honest, I shouldn't practice lying. If I want them to be kind, then I should show them what kindness looks like through my actions.

Although children are young, they are keenly aware of hypocrisy. We must do better if we want them to be better. It's unfair to expect a child to do something we adults haven't shown them how to do. In regards to relationships, the thought of my children following in my footsteps is scary. I realize now that history repeats itself. If I want a different outcome for my sons and daughters, I have to show them something different: It starts with me.

I've spent a lifetime trying to run in the opposite direction of what I saw as a child. My greatest fear was repeating the same relationship mistakes I witnessed growing up. No matter how hard I've tried not to, I seemed to have repeated them in one way or another. I know countless others who have unwillingly done the same. Not having the tools to break the cycles they learned, they end up repeating them. Nothing changes unless we change. We have the power to choose.

Looking back, I wish the women in my life would have loved themselves. Maybe then they could have been the example I needed them to be. Had they stood up for themselves and not allowed men to mistreat them, maybe I would've had the courage to do the same. I wish they would've taught me the importance of valuing myself, my body, and my own voice. I wish they would have encouraged my hopes and dreams; inspiring me to focus on and respect the woman I was becoming. Still, I hold nothing against them. I know they would have given it, if they had it to give.

This thing called self-love goes deep. We as women must come to the place where we are no longer willing to just accept what someone else gives us. We must be willing to give ourselves the love we need, so that we are not desperately seeking to get it from a relationship. We must learn to be happy outside of another person and teach our children to do the same.

# Chapter 1 Review

**Point #1:**

Your first introduction to love is important, because it affects the way in which you love. History repeats itself, but breaking the cycle of toxic relationships is possible if you are willing to do the work that is necessary.

**Point #2:**

Learning how to be happy by loving yourself first can save you from a lifetime of pain and regret. You must take the time to assess your past relationship history in order to see where you lacked self-love and accepted toxic behaviors.

**Point #3:**

God's is the source of love and through his word we learn how to love ourselves and others. When you learn to love yourself first, based upon God's love for you, it will be easier to love others in a healthy and balanced way.

# Loving the Girl in the Mirror

## 2

*If you don't learn how to love yourself first, you'll look in the mirror one day and you won't recognize the person staring back at you.*

The desire to be loved is healthy and natural, but if you are not careful you will spend your whole life striving for love instead of being loved. All you have to do is take a look at your social media feed to see that people are seeking attention and longing for acceptance. It's so easy to get caught up in the likes of others that we don't stop to ask if we like ourselves. Are we proud of our own lives?

Nobody's life is perfect, no matter how good it looks like on Instagram and Facebook. Most people are public about their highlights and silent about their heartaches, so what they show you publicly is never the whole story.

At the end of the day, it won't matter how many people liked your photo or how many virtual friends you had. The question that will either comfort or haunt you in the end is, "Was I happy with the life I chose to live?"

Only you know what it will take for you to embrace the woman in the mirror. You get to decide what's meaningful to you. Problems arise when we get so caught up in the lives of others that we no longer know what's best for us. In times like this, we must pull back and reconnect with ourselves and God.

You must become an expert at being in tune with you. We get into trouble when we expect others to know more about us than we know about ourselves. You're the only one who knows your deepest thoughts and desires. This is why you must initiate the process of learning how to become happy with who you are. Since everyone's journey is different, you can't compare yourself with others. So, accept yourself for who you are, including your flaws and all, and be happy with who God created you to be.

You can begin the process right now by saying this with me:

*I love myself. I accept myself. I will not let the mistakes of my past determine my future. I am beautiful. I am lovely. I am worthy. I am enough.*

*The life that God has for me is greater than anything I have ever imagined. I was made for more. I will have more. I decide to give myself more from this day forward. I forgive myself for the way I have treated myself and for the way I have allowed others to treat me. Please forgive me. I promise to honor you. I promise to give you the love that you deserve, and to put you first.*

# *Pieces of Me*

## Part II

Ve got married at the courthouse about six months after we
lad our first child. In my heart I knew it wasn't what I
eally wanted. By this time, the abuse had been going on
or over a year, and he had gotten into my head. He made
ne believe that I was the lowest scum of the earth. He
hought I believed I was better than him because I still
vasn't attracted to him. The truth was that he was an
overweight, slightly balding middle aged man. I wasn't
ttracted to him physically and I couldn't help that.

Deep down, I knew that I was better than him because
le lacked character. I was far from perfect, but I knew I
lidn't deserve to be treated like that.

I married him out of fear. I didn't want to live in sin because of my faith in Jesus, and I didn't want to be without my child. He had told me many times that he would kill me, if I ever tried to take his child away and I didn't doubt him for one second. He was crazy. He threatened me with knives, and on one occasion held a loaded double barrel shotgun to my head, all because I watched a video of him and his estranged son without his permission. He thrived on my fear. It's like it made him feel powerful knowing he had full control of my life. I was his slave. He was the puppet master.

The manager at the apartment complex we were staying at knew something was up and she would try to talk to me whenever she got the chance, which was rare since the only time I was allowed to leave the house alone was when I went to school. Every time she spoke to me I would brush her off and tell her that things were fine, and that I wasn't in an abusive marriage like she had been. She would tell me that things always got better temporarily before they got worse again. He had convinced me that he wasn't abusive because he never hit me with a closed fist. I believed it, but deep down I knew the truth.

I wasn't allowed to wear my hair down in public. I couldn't wear makeup. He chose the clothes that were acceptable for me to wear.

He picked out my shoes and even my winter jacket. All these still weren't enough to keep him from accusing me of cheating on him while I was at school. I tried to reason that I had no time to cheat on him. It was comical, thinking about it now. His crazed mind must have envisioned me in the bathroom stalls during my short breaks with other men. It was absolutely ridiculous.

I don't know how I managed to finish school, but by the grace of God I did. A few months before graduating with my Associates Degree, a representative from a nearby college came to talk to us about their Bachelorette Program. It was an exciting opportunity and I decided to go for it. The summer before I started the program, I found out I was six weeks pregnant.

It was an unplanned pregnancy. I was surprised, but happy. I loved being a mom. It was one of the few joys I had left in my life. Despite the setback, I started school that fall. Life went on normal for me. The abuse was normal now and I tried to not let it affect me. Being locked out of the house, having my ring taken away on a weekly basis, and walking for hours in the cold at night to escape the chaos of my life was all normal.

**To Be Continued...**

## Getting Real with Yourself

*If you don't learn to love yourself first, you'll spend your time making everyone but yourself happy.*

Getting real with yourself is hard work. Most people keep themselves so busy that they don't have time to examine the reality of their own lives. I'm guilty of this. Sometimes life can be so exhausting that distracting myself with television or scrolling senselessly through social media feels like the only relief I can find. The truth is, sometimes I don't want to be present with myself because I already know that I won't like what's there.

Honesty is hard for me, because I know that I'd have to put down the pint of Rocky Road ice cream and think about what's actually bothering me. My go-to unhealthy habit for dealing with stress is social media and sugar; maybe yours is going shopping or having too much wine. Whatever it is, you have to be willing to address negative habits in order to begin to love the girl in the mirror. It's the only way you'll become a woman you are proud of. Girl, you better learn to love yourself first!

## Do You Know You?

Who are you? What makes you happy? What makes you feel appreciated and loved, safe, and secure? Are you familiar with your strengths or just your weaknesses? Often times, women spend so much time taking care of others that they lose themselves in the process. Is that you?

Remember, you are important! Imagine caring about yourself as much as you cared for others. Imagine meeting your own needs with the same measure that you meet the needs of others. Imagine living a life you are proud of because you took the time to actually do the things you've always wanted to do, and go to places you've always wanted to go.

Now stop! Close your eyes and take twenty seconds to envision that woman, her life, and how it feels...that's the kind of life that you deserve! That's the woman you owe it to yourself to become.

## You Are Worthy of Love

Now that you realize the importance of self-love, I bet you're wondering how to practice it. Before you can begin to practice self-love, you must believe you are worthy of being loved, not just by others, but by yourself as well.

Since God is the ultimate source of love, you must believe that you were created to be loved and that you have always been loved. Believing that you are already loved will give you the motivation to begin loving yourself. Now, go ahead and have an ugly cry! Seriously, think about it for a moment. How many things have you put off doing, what places have you dared not to go, and how many relationships did you settle for, all because you felt unworthy?

I know I can admit that I've allowed thoughts of unworthiness stop me from enjoying my life to the fullest. For example, there's a very posh health food store not too far from where I live. It was built several years ago and I've heard nothing but great things about it. They have an outdoor dining area and a large assortment of organic treats I know I want to try. The problem is that the thought of going into this place intimidates the heck out of me. I know it's silly, but I have yet to get the courage to go inside. Pray for me y'all.

This may seem unreasonable, but I can't tell you how many women allow the same fear to keep them from the love they desire. They stay in unhealthy relationships for way too long and tolerate all kinds of foolish behavior from people. It's hard for them to stand up for themselves even when they know it's the right thing to do. I know this because I used to be one of these women.

'm not perfect but I'm growing and getting better every day. The last point I want to make is very important. Write t down and memorize it: If you don't believe you're worthy of "real" love, you'll never give yourself permission to have t.

## The Power of Words

*Death and life are in the power of the tongue, and those
who love it will eat its fruit.*
*-Proverbs 18:21*

As a child, I struggled with extreme shyness. I would be in class or go places, and because I was so quiet adults would iterally forget that I was there. I hated being shy, but I lidn't know how to overcome the fear of speaking up for myself in public. As a result, it was hard for me to fit in and make friends. In middle school I began to skip classes and sometimes I would act like I was going to school but actually sneak back upstairs to my room.

On one of these occasions, my mother being fed up with me called the cops. Lol. A female police officer came into my room and saw me hiding under the bed. She looked at me and left the room without saying a word. I distinctly remember hearing my mom saying, "I don't know what to do. There must be something wrong with her". I could hear the police woman agreeing and saying, "Yes, there is".

As a child, I had a deep reverence for civil servants such as firefighters and police officers. They would come to my school often to teach about drug and fire safety, so to hear that there was something wrong with me from a person I highly respected was devastating. I still remember the intense feelings of shame I experienced as I reflect on the words of that female officer.

As an adult, I now know that I have the authority to take back the power of the words the officer spoke over me that day. She didn't know me. She never even took the time to find out what was going on with me. She simply judged me.

The reality of the situation was that I was a struggling teenage girl desperately crying out for help. What I needed at that moment was understanding and grace, not judgment. That event was definitely a defining moment for me. I began to believe that there must be something wrong with me. Words are powerful! They shape our view of life and of ourselves. Similarly, they have the power to change the course of our life for better or for worse.

For a long time I allowed that experience to shape the way I viewed myself. I believed that others could see my inadequacies just as easily as the police officer did. As I learned to love myself, I realized that I didn't have to allow that situation or anyone else's opinion to define who I am. I didn't have to be stuck reliving the pain of my past. I could live free.

Today I give you permission to take back control of your life. Release yourself from the prison of shame and unworthiness. Free yourself from the chains of regret. You are not what people have said about you. Stop judging yourself by what others have done to you. Give yourself permission to accept the beautiful gift that is you.

# Chapter 2 Review

**Point #1:**

Self-love requires a willingness to be honest and open with yourself. It takes getting to know yourself, which may be hard for some due to a lost sense of identity.

**Point #2:**

Who you are as a person is important in your self-love journey. You must reignite your purpose and the dreams you once had. Becoming the woman you want to be is achievable for you, and closer than you think.

**Point #3:**

You are worthy of love. Knowing you are already loved by God is key to developing self-love. You must overcome fear, so that it doesn't hinder you from moving forward.

**Point #4:**

Words are powerful. You must take back your power from the people who have spoken negatively over you. You must decide not to allow your identity to be based upon others' opinions of you. You don't need anyone's permission to bring healing into your life through the words you speak.

# Becoming a Confident Woman

## 3

*If you don't learn how to love yourself first, you'll base your confidence on how others treat you.*

Confidence starts in your mind. It goes beyond your physical appearance and transcends any physical limitations. Let me share with you a story that a friend of mine told me.

There was a woman from his hometown in Kenya. He described her as ugly, based on the world's standards of ugliness. However, there was something about the way she carried herself that made people look at her.

She was kind, she treated other people with dignity, and she had the kind of confidence that made people's heads turn. Although she had no outward appeal, the beauty that radiated from her spirit was undeniable. She had confidence.

This story proves that confidence is not based on outward appearance, as some people think. Instead, true confidence comes from the inside out. It comes from loving yourself first, and that starts in your mind. The lady from the small town in Kenya had confidence because she knew who she was. She knew she didn't possess beauty, but what she did have was something far greater. She had learned to accept her weakness and accentuate her strengths. In doing so, she was able to radiate true beauty which comes from the heart.

Somebody once said, you can't have an unhealthy mind and live a confident life. If you want to become a confident woman, you have to develop a new mindset. Every change that has ever taken place in your life, good or bad, began in your mind. Think about a person wanting to lose weight. In order to do so, they have to envision themselves at a new and healthy weight. As they envision themselves, they begin to think about how they'll feel, the confidence they'll have, and all the things they'll be able to do. The process of envisioning is what will give them the motivation to put in the effort necessary to lose the weight.

One thing I discovered as I sought healing from my past was that I had adopted a toxic mindset from people I had been in relationships with. My self-confidence suffered because I began to define myself by the negative opinions of people who didn't genuinely know me, instead of on the truth I knew about myself. It's a dangerous thing when you let others define you. When you don't love yourself first, you'll begin to seek the approval of others. You'll care so much about what they think that you'll want to change yourself to make them happy.

Be careful because sometimes it's not you who needs to change. When you're dealing with toxic people, they'll often project their own issues on you. They will make you believe that you're the problem when it's actually their own insecurities.

You'll end up confused; trying to fix problems that don't exist because you were never the issue. It's crazy when you think about it, but the old saying is true: hurting people hurt people. Don't be one of their casualties. Trust your intuition and leave the relationship if the person isn't willing to change. This includes family relationships. No one is worth risking your sanity and peace over.

When I recognized that my thoughts and opinions were a result of things that others impressed upon me, I was upset. I was angry that I had allowed others to control and manipulate me. I was angry because I played the fool. I had to learn how to separate my own voice from the voice of others. I had to regain my self-confidence. As I learned to silence the lies and negative voices in my head, I simultaneously learned to honor my own voice.

I began to reject the negative thoughts and replace them with positive ones. I had to relearn how to trust myself again, because I had been made to believe that I was incapable of making good decisions for myself and needed someone to make them for me.

It will take time, but as you distance yourself from toxic people you will begin to recognize the negative thought patterns and begin to change them. Toxic relationships can take a serious toll on your mental health and self-confidence. It's vital that you learn how to think in a healthy way so you can develop confidence. You must learn to shift your mind from negative to positive.

# Pieces of Me

## Part III

I had genetic testing done early on in my pregnancy. The doctor called me with the results and told me that there was a high possibility that my son would have Down Syndrome and they would watch his growth throughout my pregnancy. I told him the news when he came home, and he told me that I shouldn't keep it because most marriages don't survive with kids who have special needs. I was disgusted by his disregard for human life. I didn't care whether or not I had to parent this child alone; I knew that I would never get an abortion. The conversation was never brought up again.

The physical and emotional abuse continued throughout the pregnancy. One evening, I was feeling in the mood, and for whatever reason he wasn't interested. He usually only wanted to be intimate when I didn't want to be. I later found out that this tactic is also a form of emotional abuse called withholding. When I saw that he didn't want to be together, I was visibly upset. I don't remember what I did or said, but next thing I know I'm being dragged by my hair across the bedroom floor at seven months pregnant.

After the incident, a patch of hair was missing from the front of my head and my bra strap was ripped. Once again, I was shocked and helpless. I was afraid for my life. All the power I had to stand up for myself was gone. The thought of calling the cops was the farthest thing from my mind. In the black culture, we are usually discouraged from calling the police. Men in uniform are viewed as the bad ones. Maybe this internalized view of law enforcement was what prevented me from calling for help.

The next day, I was set to do my final ultrasound before giving birth. I was upset about what happened and like usual he never apologized. I was often told that I had to forgive, because I was a Christian. It's funny how people have double standards. They hold other people at a standard they themselves are unwilling to keep. We went to that appointment and acted like nothing had happened.

By this time I had had about four ultrasounds. Each time, they would measure the limbs and other parts of the body to see if they were consistent with other children who had the disability. Each time, I would come home with tons of new pics and uncertain results. This appointment was the same. I got more ultrasound pictures and was told that he looked good, but they just wouldn't be able to tell if he had Down Syndrome until he was born.

I waited anxiously for my due date. It came and went. I was miserable and ready. Two days later, around 3am on March 2, 2009, I woke up to intense contractions. I had some mild ones earlier that day, but they fizzled out by midday. From having my previous child, I knew these were the real deal. I grabbed my back and we hopped in the car and headed to the hospital. Unlike my first child, we had a vehicle this time.

During my first labor, we walked about a mile and a half to the bus station, took a 30 minute ride downtown, and walked about another 10 minutes to the hospital from the bus stop, all while I was in active labor. After finally being checked in and getting a room, the nurse checked me and told me that I was fully dilated. I was shocked when she told me to start pushing.

I had heard horror stories of giving birth, so naturally I was fearful. The anesthesiologist was sleeping when I arrived so they had to wake him up. After waiting for another 45 minutes, he finally came and made three attempts to give me an epidural.

When he couldn't get it in, I just told them I would give birth naturally. She came out in about three pushes on Father's Day, June 17, 2007. It really wasn't that bad. I didn't experience the ring of fire so many women talk about. I was amazed at the strength of my own body. I was a mother.

I've been told that I have a high pain tolerance. I guess this is true because when I got to the hospital for the birth of my son, my second child, I was already 8 ½ centimeters dilated. I went natural again with no pain medication. When it came time to push, I pushed about five times and he was stuck.

I was exhausted, so the doctor decided to suction his head to help him come out. With help, he slid right out. He was as white as a Caucasian, with a big head and short stubby legs. My first thought was that he was going to be a midget. Lol. The best news of all was that he was happy and healthy. He didn't have Down Syndrome.

I enjoyed the time in the hospital. Being taken care of was a treatment I wasn't used to. I was there for a day when my ex told me he wanted me to go home. I didn't want to because I liked it there at the hospital. I knew as soon as I got home I would have to start cooking and cleaning right away. He was so selfish. He couldn't stand to see me happy and enjoying myself for a minute.

I told him I didn't want to go, but when he persisted I knew to just agree with him and go; so that's what we did. Just as I suspected, he just wanted me home to be his maid. It was all about him. He began his controlling behaviors again, telling me when I could and couldn't breastfeed my son.

We went to his mother's house that November for Thanksgiving. She was elderly and I could tell she never really liked me. He had this love hate relationship with women that stemmed from his mother. It was really awkward. During our time there, we stayed in her room and she slept in her chair in the living room.

He refused to let me breastfeed my son for about two days straight. I was engorged and in great pain. I couldn't sit up and I could barely walk because the pain was so great from the amount of milk that filled my breasts. I was angry, but I knew I couldn't cross him. I knew his mom would be on his side no matter what and I didn't doubt he would hit me in her presence. I begged him with tears in my eyes to let me feed my son.

Finally, on the last day we were there he agreed to let me breastfeed again. I was so happy to have the relief as my son nursed. I was so engorged that it took a few days of my son nursing for my breasts to return to normal. That man was evil. There was no Christ inside of him. He was a monster.

**To Be Continued...**

# The Shame & Blame Mindset

In order to develop confidence you must overcome a negative mindset. One unhealthy mindset is shame and blame. People can get stuck in this mindset when they've been through traumatic experiences they've not healed from. When you're operating in this mindset you carry around negative energy. You relive the pain you've experienced daily and you struggle with anger, depression, and sometimes post traumatic stress disorder. How do I know? I lived this.

When you experience trauma, it affects your mind. The way you view yourself and others becomes distorted. Many people have had bad things happen to them that are not their fault such as childhood sexual abuse, neglect, rape, intimate partner violence aka domestic violence, adultery, divorce, and more.

Experiencing these things is terrible and can leave you with unhealed scars. If you don't learn to heal from your pain, it will hinder your ability to grow and progress in life. Don't allow your past to hold you back from the life that God wants for you. You don't have to be a victim of your past. You don't have to carry the shame of what others have done to you.

You have the God-given ability to choose and to change. Below are steps that I have personally used to heal from my past.

1. Forgive yourself

2. Forgive the offender(s)

3. Accept responsibility for your "now"

4. Seek professional help to overcome your past/pain

5. Be consistent

6. Keep yourself in a positive environment/people

7. Continue to walk out self-love daily

Forgiveness is a hard one for many. If you don't have the right perspective on forgiveness, it seems unjust. If you don't understand that forgiveness is about setting yourself free, then you'll struggle with it for the rest of your life. Often times, the people that have abused or betrayed us have moved on with their lives, while the ones that they've hurt are still suffering from the consequences of their behavior.

People who hold on to bitterness and unforgiveness can suffer physical ailments and life-threatening diseases because of the stress resulting from the trauma.

## The Learning & Growth Mindset

The learning and growth mindset is something you must develop in order to move forward in life. Many times our way of thinking keeps us stuck in toxic cycles. You have to develop healthy attitudes and new habits in order to become a confident woman. The learning and growth mindset happens when you begin to be proactive and create solutions for your situation instead of allowing shame and blame to hinder you. It's when you assume responsibility for your future that you take back your power.

You can begin to operate in this mindset through this list of things to do:

- *Develop a ready to learn attitude.* In order to grow, you must be willing to learn. Don't be too proud to take good advice. Listen to wisdom.

- *Seek out understanding and new knowledge.* If you want to go to a place you've never been to, then find someone who's been there and learn from them. You can easily find a virtual mentor via YouTube, podcasts, and blogs. There's no excuse to stay in the same place because there are millions of people in the world with the knowledge to help you get to your next level.

- *Be honest with yourself.* If you want to have confidence, you must be honest with yourself, who you are, your mistakes, and what you want from life. No one gets to decide your life but you. Don't sell yourself short by trying to live someone else's dream or copy another person's life. You deserve a life that makes you happy. You only get one, so live it well.

- *Receive constructive criticism graciously.* Many people who struggle with low self-confidence take everything personally. Realizing that this way of existing is unhealthy and counterproductive to growth is necessary. Every person has areas they can improve upon. The key is to separate who you are from what you do. Knowing that your value isn't dependent on performance but on the eternal love of God makes everything a little sweeter.

- *Examine and analyze your past and learn from it.* If you don't learn from the past, you are doomed to repeat it. You must be willing to face the pain of your past and find healing if you want to move forward. The quality of your future depends on the decisions you make today. Don't waste your pain; let it have purpose. Be willing to learn the lessons and receive the wisdom of life, so that you don't have to repeat them.

## Loving The Skin You're In

You can become a confident woman. You don't have to be the perfect size, or be in a romantic relationship. Remember that confidence is birthed from within. If you don't learn how to love yourself first, you'll never be confident because there will always be something else that you think you need to achieve in order to attain it.

I remember when I was fifteen. I was 127lbs and I thought I was overweight. I didn't like myself and I spent most of my time seeking attention and acceptance. I struggled with eating disorders and low self-esteem. I look back at old pictures of myself and I think I was crazy because I looked amazing. You see, when you compare yourself to others you'll never feel good enough, because no matter how hard you try, you'll never be able to be somebody else.

I had to learn how to love myself regardless of my weight, skin color, and hair texture. I struggled a lot growing up because in my mind I wasn't beautiful. I thought that in order to be beautiful, I had to be thin with blonde hair and blue eyes or mixed with light skin, long wavy hair, and a body like a pop star. It didn't help that I was a little chunky with a butt that kids would make fun of.

My mom was also really light-skinned. I used to pray and hope that my skin would lighten overnight, and that I would be skinny like the other girls at school. It seemed that everyone had boys feigning over them except me. I struggled with these insecurities into adulthood and it has been reflected in all of my relationships. I settled for men who I didn't like out of fear, hoping that maybe, just maybe they'd love me. It turns out that all I needed to do was love myself.

Through the years, I have learned through trial and error how to honor and love myself. I have by no means arrived. It's a daily practice and a life-long journey. What I have learned I want to share with you in the hopes that you will find freedom and receive the revelation of how amazing you truly are. Below are the things I've done and will continue to do to be a confident woman.

- *Forgive Yourself.* In order to be confident I had to forgive myself for all the mistakes I had made. I couldn't become confident beating myself up everyday over all my regrets. I had to ask myself for forgiveness for settling for less, so that I could then give myself permission to have better. This was not a one-time thing. I had to do this daily sometimes. As you begin to do this over time you'll have to do it less and less, and you'll find it easier to forgive yourself.

- ***Work with What You Got.*** You'll never be confident hoping and wishing you were somebody else. There comes a time when you have to accept yourself as you are. If there's something you want to change that's realistic such as: losing weight, dressing better, or getting a new hairstyle, then go for it. Just make sure you're doing it with the right motives. Nothing can make you more worthy of love; remember your value comes from God. Improve yourself because you want to be the best version of yourself, not to please others. Refuse to believe that you have to be like somebody else. You are unique and God created you as you are for a reason, so you might as well love you.

- ***Surround Yourself with Greatness.*** You can't be great hanging around small-minded people. I've heard it said that if you look at your five closest friends, that's where you'll be in five years. It's vital to watch the company that you keep, because you'll become like those you hang out with the most. It may sound terrifying if you're shy like me, but you have to branch out and find people who inspire, elevate, and challenge you to be better.

The bible also has a lot to say about the friends you hang out with:

*As iron sharpens iron, so a friend sharpens a friend.*
*-Proverbs 27:17 (NLT)*

*Do not be deceived: Bad company corrupts good morals.*
**-1 Corinthians 15:33**

*Make no friendship with an angry man, and with a furious man do not go, Lest you learn his ways and set a snare for your soul.*
**-Proverbs 22: 24-25**

*Confidence in an unfaithful man in time of trouble is like a bad tooth and a foot out of joint.*
**-Proverbs 25:19**

# Chapter 3 Review

**Point #1:**

Becoming a confident woman starts in your mind. True confidence isn't based on outward circumstances, but on loving and accepting yourself as you are. The road to self-confidence takes work and honesty, but it's worth it.

**Point #2:**

Developing a confidence mindset starts with addressing any negative thought patterns that you have. You can't be confident if your mind is unhealthy. Address your thoughts and replace negativity with positivity.

**Point #3:**

Learning and growing is a part of moving forward. Becoming the woman you want to be takes a readiness to acquire new knowledge, being honest, and the ability to receive constructive criticism and learn from your past.

**Point #4:**

Accepting yourself as you are and improving yourself will help build your confidence. You must also learn to forgive yourself, work with what you have, and surround yourself with greatness. The company you keep affects your destiny, so choose wisely.

# Creating Healthy Relationships

## 4

***If you don't learn how to love yourself first, you'll have relationships with people who treat you like an enemy more than a friend.***

The impact that a single person can have on another's life is humbling. If you're blessed enough to be surrounded by loving, caring, trustworthy people, count yourself blessed! Unfortunately, most people haven't had this experience. How many people have you let into your life who turned out to be someone other than who you thought they were?

How many times have you held on to one-sided relationships, out of fear, that didn't benefit you? So many people have had their lives disrupted, downgraded, and devastated by people who they thought they could trust. The best relationship wisdom I can give you is this: *Not everyone deserves the privilege of your presence.*

As you learn to love yourself first, you'll realize the importance of creating healthy relationships. The longer you live, the more you'll accept that not everyone has earned a seat at your table. The first key to having healthy relationships is to accept the fact that not everyone from your past is fit for your future. The second key is to make sure you're walking in your purpose, because if you don't know who you are, then you won't know who you need.

You must become an expert at knowing yourself. Who am I? Where am I going? What do I want out of life? After you sit down with yourself and write down these things, the next thing you will need to do is stop worrying about what others think of you. You will never be able to please everyone.

Caring about those who are closest to you and the people you love is healthy, but worrying about the opinions of strangers and people who are not a part of your inner circle is a waste of time. When it comes down to it, only you can decide what you want and need in your life.

*He who walks with wise men will be wise, But the companion of fools will be destroyed.*
***-Proverbs 13:20***

Another important thing that you must do to create healthy relationships is become a people watcher. You've heard the saying, "Actions speak louder than words". If a person is true and genuine, then what they say and do will line up. Ask yourself these questions as you think about the relationships you already have in your life:

- How do they make me feel?

- Do they celebrate me?

- Do they comfort me when I suffer loss?

- Are they supportive?

- Do they encourage me to be my best self?

- Is my life better because they're in it?

- Are they trustworthy?

- Is the relationship mutual or one-sided?

- What does my gut feeling tell me about this person?

- Can I envision this person in the future I want for myself?

This self-love journey may seem self-centered at first, but there's no point in having people in your life who hold you back and make you miserable. How many people do you know who are in long-term relationships with people they don't like, can't trust, and who bring them down? The people we allow into our lives should make our lives better. Life is hard enough without the added frustration of having people in our lives who only bring us pain.

Your journey to self-love can't be about anyone else but you. When you learn to love yourself first, you'll allow people into your life who have proven that they deserve to be there. Remember that this takes time. People get into so much trouble because they're impatient and don't want to wait for things. I'm a living witness to this.

As you learn to love yourself first, you will begin to intentionally surround yourself with people that love you and celebrate you. You deserve to be more than tolerated by people who say they love you. It may seem hard at first, but it will get easier as you do it more and more. Your life will begin to flourish because there will be no one holding you back from being the greatest version of yourself.

# Pieces of Me

## Part IV

stayed for the kids. I was afraid of how they'd suffer if I wasn't around. Although he made sure their physical needs were met, he had a mean streak and would often discipline the kids way above and beyond what was age appropriate or humane. I wanted to take pictures of the bruises he left on their little bodies so many times, but I knew if he ever found them there would be hell to pay. He would spank them just for crying sometimes. The first time I tried to intervene, he told me that he would kill me if I ever got between him and his children again. The look on his face told me he was serious.

I was furious so many times. How did I get here? Why was God allowing this to happen to me? How could he get away with treating me like this? Did God really hate women and favor men as it seemed? I wanted to be close to God, but I was angry at him for allowing this man to mistreat me. If he was God he could stop it, and he didn't so he must be okay with it. How could I get close to a God I thought hated me?

Sometimes we went to church, never for long though. As soon as we found one I loved he would find something about it to critique: the music was too emotional, the pastor's sermon wasn't good, or his favorite, I have more knowledge of the bible than the pastor. He loved to brag and boast about himself. Too bad he couldn't see what an arrogant jerk he was.

Everyone he knew was in awe of him and thought he could do no wrong. Everywhere we went, people who he introduced me to would sing his praise, stating how I was so lucky to have him. If they only knew what I knew, but of course he would never let anyone see that. His true nature was only revealed to those he knew he could manipulate and have control over; everyone else was fooled.

His mother thought he was the best thing; of course as mothers do. I tried to make the best of the few occasions we were allowed to visit her, as messed up as it was, because they were the only family I had during that time.

There was one holiday when we visited with the children and my youngest son was under one at the time and barely crawling. I don't remember what got my ex upset, but he began to embarrass me in front of his mother and told her personal and intimate details about our relationship. I was humiliated and wasn't going to sit there and let him ridicule me in front of her and our children. I started gathering my things to leave and he came over and took away my keys and purse.

It was pouring down rain outside and I don't think I even took a jacket with me. I didn't care. His mother's house was over four and a half miles from where we stayed, but I was determined to gather the little self-respect I did have left and exit stage right. So, on a dark rainy night, on a holiday that should've been filled with fun and family, I walked for miles in the dark to get home.

It was cold and I could barely see because the rain was coming down so hard. I took frequent stops at bus stops to rest and orientate myself. It took me two and a half hours to get home, my feet felt like heavy weights, and my body was sore. As I approached the door, I could see that it was open. He was there waiting for me. He shook me down roughly like a cop searching for drugs, then left. He and the children were gone for three days. I was so relieved to not have to worry about him. I could rest and be at peace until he returned.

***To Be Continued...***

# Believe What People Show You

The best advice I've ever heard about relationships is from the late poet Maya Angelou, "When people show you who you are, believe them the first time". I wish that I could say I heard this advice one time and it stuck. Unfortunately, I've had to suffer through a lot of pain and a few abusive relationships before I learned this lesson.

As women, we like to believe that we have the power to love someone into changing. We think that our love is more powerful than Jesus. We put ourselves in dangerous places trying to make people be who we want them to be instead of who they really are. Let me free you sista: If someone doesn't want to change, then they won't, and there is nothing you can do about it.

No amount of ultimatums, bargaining, yelling, praying, and hoping is enough to change someone who doesn't want to change. This fact was very hard for me to accept. Instead of believing what people showed me, I stubbornly believed that I could force someone to change. The truth of the matter is: you can think you're helping someone when you're actually hindering them.

I stayed in an extremely toxic relationship for years thinking that if I forgave enough, was kind enough and stood by them, they would eventually snap out of it, see me for the wonderful person I was, and love me in return.

The reality was that the more crap I put up with, the more forgiving I was; and the more boundaries I allowed them to break, the more disrespect they showed me and the less love I received. It won't work sis. You must believe people when they show you who they are. Learning to release toxic people is the best gift you can give yourself.

## What You Allow Will Continue

Like many lessons, I had to learn this one the hard way. I once believed that verbally disagreeing with someone's behavior was enough to stand my ground. I believed that I was powerless beyond this, and that I had to just accept other's behavior. What a lie. When you begin to love yourself first, you will begin to see that you have more power and influence than you realize.

Unfortunately, most people will do what they can get away with. A speaker I greatly respect tells the story of how he was a toxic and immature man when he met his wife. He says that his wife was the first woman who stood her ground and didn't allow him to mistreat, control, and manipulate her. She left him once during dating and once during marriage because he failed to live up to the standards she knew she deserved.

I've never witnessed a man speak so respectfully and affectionately about his wife the way this man does. He credits his wife's no nonsense attitude for helping him develop into the man he is today.

When it comes to relationships, actions speak louder than words. When someone continually mistreats you, and you allow that person to stay in your life, you are condoning their behavior with your presence. In order to have healthy relationships you must demand to be treated with a certain level of respect. You have to overcome your fear of being rejected and alone. It is far better to be alone and at peace, than to be surrounded by people who despise and disrespect you.

People who don't respect your boundaries or wishes don't love or respect you. I don't think that's the type of relationship any of us want to have. That's not the kind of relationship that God desires for you to have. As God's daughter, he wants the very best for you, and you must come to a place where you want the very best for you too.

## Let Them Lose You

As women, we must learn to master our emotions so that we make decisions based on logic and not fear. One thing that is helpful is to look at your situation from the outside.

Imagine your best friend being in the same situation, and then give yourself advice from that place. You have to give yourself permission to have better, be better, and do better. Stop placing your happiness in the hands of other people.

Your life is too important to allow someone else to mishandle it. If someone is unwilling to give you what you need, you have to be willing to let them go and love them from a distance. You must learn to love yourself first, if you ever expect someone else to give you the love you desire.

One reason we have a hard time letting go of unhealthy relationships is because we're holding on to the slim chance that one day things might change. How many times does someone have to be unfaithful to you? How many times do they need to disrespect you? How many times does someone have to tell you that they don't want you? We want to give people the benefit of the doubt, but often times it ends up coming back to bite us.

You need to see yourself differently. You are loved. You are valuable. You do deserve the best. When you begin to see yourself like this, it will be easier to walk away from people who don't value you. You must refuse to compromise your dignity and self-respect for another person. *People who deserve to be a part of your life will do what's necessary to stay a part of your life.*

You must understand something: people who love and respect you won't constantly violate your boundaries. You may have to tell a person once, at the most twice, but after that you're just playing the fool. Trust me; I have learned the hard way because I'm very stubborn. People who love you are concerned about your well being and won't intentionally do things to hurt you.

Of course everyone makes mistakes, but remember that repeated offenses are choices not mistakes. Shift your thinking and begin to see losing the people in your life who don't treat you right as gain and not a loss.

## Picky on Purpose

*If you don't learn how to love yourself first, you'll let people into your life without ever asking yourself if they should be there.*

Being picky is usually seen as a negative thing, but in the context of choosing the people who you want in your life, it is a necessary thing. Knowing that you have the power to choose is an amazing feeling. A lot of people are stripped of their power because they feel hopeless to change their situation. They learn to accept whatever life throws their way. You don't have to live like this anymore.

You don't have to be pessimistic about life because you're afraid of being disappointed again. God has promised good things for those who love him. It's time to start believing again. Now let's take a look at some different examples of incompatible relationships to see why it's important to be selective in your relationships.

**Example #1:**

You are a positive person who always sees the bright side of life. You thrive on positive energy and inspiring people. Would it be wise to make friendships with negative people who are pessimistic about life?

**Example #2:**

You are a very hard working, ambitious person with big plans for the future. Would it be a good move to make friends with someone who has no drive and no goals in life? Is there a chance they could discourage you? They may want you to stay on the same level as them because they're happy there and they think you should be too.

**Example #3:**

You are a responsible person. You pay your bills on time, and are good at managing your finances. You're working hard to get out of debt and save money for retirement. Would it be smart for you to date someone who is financially irresponsible?

(a person that frequently maxes out his/her credit cards, spends money on getting her hair done, and lives a generally careless life?)

## Example #4

You are an outgoing, high-energy person. You like to go out on adventures, travel, meet new people, and try new things on a weekly basis. While out one day you meet someone you find very attractive. He seems family-oriented, has a fulfilling career, and makes good money.

However, after a few dates you find out that he is very reserved, doesn't like to travel, and avoids meeting new people at all costs. What do you do? Most people would be optimistic thinking that they could change that person, and that is possible; but as people get older they usually get stuck in their ways and don't want to change. You don't want to end up marrying a person for who you want them to be, instead of who they really are.

I hope that you're beginning to see more clearly why it's so important to choose your relationships wisely. Many people have had their lives altered in ways they could've never imagined, all because of the people they allowed in it. Think about all the people serving prison sentences because they were with a person who committed a crime. Unfair as it may seem, you will be affected by the people you allow into your life.

I know some people probably think that it's not that serious, but those are usually the same people who are stuck in life because they don't have any goals and have allowed others to hinder them. They are generally negative people who haven't accomplished much in life. Sorry, if that's you. The bible has this to say about the company we keep:

*Don't fool yourselves. Bad friends will destroy you.*
*-1 Corinthians 15:33 (CSB)*

There comes a point in your life where you have to stop caring what others think of you more than you care about what you think about you. Unfortunately, some people never get to a place of self-reflection and change for the better. What kind of person do you want to be? Is it worth it to live life, fearing what others think about you? Girl, you deserve better. You better go get it!

## Love is on the Other Side of Fear

*If you don't learn how to love yourself first, you'll let the attitudes and opinions of others control you.*

I can't tell you how many times I've been afraid to let go of relationships out of fear. Maybe it was the fear of being alone, the fear of failure, or the fear of not being able to find anyone better. I regret every one of those decisions.

The best decisions I've made in my life have been based on logic, sound reasoning, and what I intuitively knew was best for me at the time. Fear is bondage.

When you learn how to make choices aside from your emotions you will discover that they are some of the best choices that you've ever made. Emotions have the ability to cloud our judgment and make us irrational. When we take the emotions out of the decisions we make, we can see clearly to find solutions. What choices have you made out of fear? Are you happy with those choices or do you regret them? Did you know that you cannot make choices based on love if you are operating in fear? Here's why.

*There is no fear in love; but perfect love casts out fear, because fear involves torment. But he who fears has not been made perfect in love.*
**-1 John 4:18**

According to the scripture above, the choices we make out of fear will torment us. God created us for peace. Fear is the opposite of peace, because it creates anxiety and mental anguish. It may take time, but it's possible for you to live your life free from fear. I'm still a work-in-progress, but everyday I'm learning how to be still, so that I can make sound decisions that I don't have to regret later on down the road.

From now on you can choose the people who you want in our life from a place of love, self-love. You get to decide who and what's best for you. I'm so proud of you. I know you can do it!

# Chapter 4 Review

**Point #1:**

Not everyone deserves the privilege of your presence. Your closest relationships should serve a purpose. They should be mutually beneficial and good for your health and well-being.

**Point #2:**

What you allow will continue. Your presence condones bad behavior, even when your mouth condemns it. You teach people with your actions, not your words. You must let go of people who are unwilling to raise their standards.

**Point #3:**

Believe what people show you, not what they tell you. People are who they are, and wishing that they were different won't change anything. We cannot change others, but we can change ourselves. Be willing to let go of relationships that are not mutual or unhealthy in nature, without feeling guilty. It's okay to love people from a distance.

**Point #4:**

Care more about what you think about you, than what others do. You don't have time to worry about what other people think. Keep busy pursuing your goals and your dreams.

**Point #5:**

Compatibility is often an overlooked aspect of relationships. You may want them to go with you, but can they grow with you? You cannot allow fear to keep you tied to people who are not good for you. You deserve people in your life who add value to it, and who celebrate you. Love is on the other side of fear. The genuine relationships you desire aren't as far away as you think.

# Do You Lack Standards?

## 5

*If you don't learn how to love yourself first, you'll lower your standards for people who don't have any.*

Setting standards for yourself is extremely important because they let you know what you're willing to accept. Standards are like guardrails that protect you from going in the wrong direction. When you begin to get off course they help get you back on the right track. Over the years I can see how I lowered my standards thinking that it would make a relationship work out.

I made excuses for people instead of requiring them to change. I tried to change myself and only ended up making matters worse. I have been in relationships where I thought I could try enough for the both of us. Boy bye! Ain't nobody got time for that! I laugh now thinking about it. As we age I think we have less tolerance for foolish behavior, because we realize that we don't have a lot of time left and we want to enjoy what we do have.

At the age of thirty four, peace is my priority and I'm unwilling to make exceptions. I'm thankful that I am able to look back and learn from my mistakes, although it's sad to say that many people cannot say the same. I know people twice my age still doing the same things they did in their twenties and thirties. There comes a point in life where we should be learning, growing, and getting better. You can't claim ignorance forever.

I remember a dream I had after going through a rough time in a relationship. I was angry at God for not revealing things to me that could have kept me out of the relationship. I was so angry because I thought I did everything right. In the dream a friend of mine spoke to me and said, "You may not have known about it then, but now you do. What are you going to do about it?" When I woke up from the dream I knew that God was speaking to me concerning the situation.

The dream taught me to take back ownership of my life. I had to take my power back. You may not know why God allows certain things in our lives, but you have to make the decision to get back up. You can't go back and change the past, but you have the power to change right now. I love this quote by C.S. Lewis:

*You can go back and change the beginning, but you can start where you are and change the ending.*

You are not asking for too much in your relationships, you just may be asking for it from the wrong people. Sometimes we lower our standards thinking that people can't meet them, when in reality they refuse to. We think we're helping them when we are actually hurting ourselves and robbing them of an opportunity to grow. Stepping away from the relationship may be what they really need to face reality and finally grow up.

Please don't allow a grown adult to convince you that mutual love, respect, and faithfulness is too high of a demand. If a wild animal such as a lion or gorilla can learn to tame their beastly nature and behave in a gentle way with their caretakers, then a fully grown human can do what's needed as well. Do yourself a favor and hold tight to your standards and expectations. If you don't have any, it's time to get some.

# Pieces of Me

Part V

Our apartment manager finally had gotten tired of our neighbors calling the police on us because of the constant yelling and dishes being thrown against the wall. She gave us a warning and told us that the next time they were called, I would have to leave because he was on section eight before we got married, and was the head of the household. I thought that was stupid, but what could I do? I felt helpless yet again.

I had no money because I wasn't working and was in school full time, plus all of the extra money was taken and hidden by him.

When I got pregnant with our first daughter, he made me start taking out student loans instead of him getting a job. My entire life I had avoided debt because I had witnessed people close to me suffer as a result of it. I vowed to never get a credit card or owe people money. I was always good at saving money. Now I was left feeling completely stupid. He had abused me, taken my money, and now I was about to be homeless without my children, all while attending school full time.

The day finally came when the police were called for the last time and she told me I had a few days to move out. I was lost and had no place to go. My pride wouldn't let me call my mother after being estranged for years because I didn't want to be seen as a failure. My family didn't even know I had any children. I hadn't seen any of them for years. I especially missed my nieces and nephews because I was always close to them. They were like my children before I became a mom.

Through some God-orchestrated event, my ex found a homeless house for women that I could move to. The only thing was that it was a recovery home for women who had been on drugs. I was scared because I didn't know what to expect. I didn't really have other options. The rent was cheap and it was a safe place to lay my head. I knew that I wouldn't be there long, so I agreed.

The first night was the hardest because it was the first time I'd ever been away from my children. To my surprise, the women were normal women just like you and me. They had just made some bad decisions and gotten involved with the wrong crowd. I even befriended a few of the women, and although I no longer see them I still think of them sometimes.

There was no phone in the house, so I had to walk a few blocks to use the pay phone. I remember calling that night and asking him to talk to the children, but he wouldn't let me. I felt hopeless and I wanted to die. I felt that my children were all I had left in this world and if I didn't have them there was no reason for me to live. I walked back home feeling defeated.

The next day at my school, we were having group presentations for our end of the semester projects. One of the groups did a project on children, so in their video presentation there was nothing but children. I cried on the inside. No one knew what I was going through. I couldn't talk to anyone. I had been so brainwashed that I just suffered in silence, as usual.

Despite the emotional pain, things started to turn around for me. I had more freedom than I had in years. I got a library card and spent most days there doing assignments and renting books and movies.

He also started bringing the kids by on the weekends. It was at that same time, less than a month from the time I moved to the shelter, when I began making plans to get a one bedroom apartment. This intimidated my ex.

I don't think he expected me to get myself together so quickly. He started ridiculing and mocking me about my plans and how I was getting closer to God.

He would curse at me while I did our daughter's hair before she left for the week. I would just sit there and sing praises to God. It made him so furious that he couldn't get to me anymore. He couldn't control me. I had control of my own money now. I could do what I wanted with my time.

I even got a work study job at the Boys and Girls Club paying seventeen dollars an hour. It was only part time, but I was feeling better than I had in years. In a few weeks I would be in my own place. I would have my privacy again. I could have my friends over.

In all my excitement I was still concerned about my ex because I knew he would find out where I lived as soon as he dropped the kids off. Although I didn't know how I would handle him, I was just happy to be getting on my feet.

While working at the Boys & Girls Club I found out that my niece and nephew attended there. It had been so long since I had seen them that I barely recognized them.

When I asked a fellow employee if their names were Deontre & Avoni and she said yes, I cried. I had missed them so much. I also reunited with my sister, Nicole, that evening when she came to pick them up. Shortly after, I reconnected with my mom. She met her grandchildren for the first time and fell in love. God was restoring things. A few weeks after starting my job, I had to quit because of a life threatening event.

**To Be Continued...**

# What Is it Costing You?

*If you don't learn how to love yourself first, you'll allow others to mistreat you out of fear of losing them.*

People appreciate what they have to work for. Just think about it. If someone gave you a brand new car, you'd happily take it without thinking of the price. Now imagine seeing the car of your dreams. It's brand new, shiny, and it has everything you ever wanted in a vehicle. You don't have the money up front so you take a second job and work double shifts.

On your days off you drive Uber and save up for a whole year. At the end of the year you count your money and discover that you have enough to buy the car and be debt free. You go to the dealership with a smile on your face, sign the papers, and the car is yours.

Now, what would you appreciate more: the car that was given to you, or the car that you had to work hard for and earn? I know that I would appreciate more the car I worked for because every time I see it and drive it, I would be reminded of the price I paid for it.

When was the last time someone had to work for you? Do you require a person, romantically speaking, to sacrifice for you and demonstrate his love to you or are you so desperate that you just jump in head first before you even know who he is? I know I'm guilty of going all in and asking questions later.

As I look back on both of the toxic relationships I was in, there were already red flags from the very beginning. In his book, The Father Daughter Talk, Bishop R.C Blakes says this: "Those playing a role will eventually forget their part". In other words, it's only a matter of time before a person shows you his real character. The problem is that we rush into relationships so fast, that by the time we find out the truth about a person, our hearts and bodies are already involved. Girl, you need to stop selling yourself short.

One thing that I've noticed about women is that we give way too much, too soon, that we end up being taken for granted, taking advantage of, and just plain used. When the relationships turn sour we scratch our heads wondering what went wrong. Usually, a person never appreciated us because we never taught them how to. It's like the person who received the free car and gladly took what was offered, but the feelings were never mutual.

Most of us believe that people are generally good. We think that because we have good intentions, others must have them too. However, there are plenty of people who have no problem using others for what they can get, and then quickly move on.

How often do you stop to ask yourself in the beginning what you want out of relationships? How often do you think about how you will conduct yourself in relationships? Do you take the time to evaluate whether a relationship is worthy of your time or not?

For me, I know that I have made assumptions about people and given credit where it wasn't due. If you want to have happy, healthy relationships you must set expectations up front. It cannot be left to another person to read your mind or know what you want and need. It is your job, because it is your life! Stop expecting people to treat you the way you think you deserve to be treated.

You must demand to be treated in a certain way. I'm not saying that you should be rude and arrogant, but as a human being, you deserve to have healthy, reciprocal relationships with people who love and value you. Not having standards will cost you everything, and everything is too high of a price to pay. Don't lose your dignity and your identity trying to make others love you.

## Letting Go of the Past

For those who feel like they've made too many mistakes, letting go of the past can be extremely difficult. Reflecting on the past is beneficial when done with the objective of learning and growing from it; but replaying it in your mind out of shame and regret will only lead to mental and emotional anguish.

So many people, including me, have held themselves hostage to their past mistakes.

Long after the experience is over and others have moved on, they continue to live with the sorrow and disappointment of their actions. Please don't do this to yourself. It's tempting to replay how you think things could have and should have gone, but in the end, it gets you nowhere. No one has the power to change the past.

Constantly looking back will only hinder you from moving forward with your life. Everyone has something they wish they had done differently. Everyone has something they wish they could go back to and change. You're not alone. One thing that really helped me was to see my past from a different perspective. Instead of viewing my mistakes through the lenses of shame and regret, I made the choice to start seeing them as teaching tools. Experience is the greatest teacher, because some lessons can only be learned through experience.

Think about a young toddler. He's been walking for a few weeks and is confident and ready to explore. He goes into the kitchen and his mother tells him not to touch the stove because it's hot. He tests her by touching it, only to find out that it's not hot like she says. What he doesn't understand is that it's only hot when something is cooking in it.

The next day, while his mother is baking cookies, he excitedly enters the kitchen.

His mom reminds him not to touch the stove because it's hot, and the cookies aren't ready yet. When his mother looks away, the boy reaches out his hand to touch the hot stove and burns himself before his mother can stop him. He screams in pain and his mother comforts him as she tends to the mild burn. After he is soothed, she tells the child that he needs to listen to her and that he should never ever touch the oven again because she doesn't want him to get hurt.

The boy listens this time because he has felt the pain of the hot oven. He has learned from his own experience that touching the hot stove brings pain. Similarly, sometimes we have to experience the pain of our choices in order to learn from them. Making mistakes is a part of being human. It's when we fail to learn from our mistakes that we suffer the most. Learn to see your mistakes as learning opportunities instead of failures. You can do this by asking yourself the following questions:

1. What did the experience teach me?

2. What have I learned about others?

3. What did I discover about myself?

4. Is there anything I need to change? Why or why not?

5. Was my experience a result of a lack of self-love?

6. Did I ignore the red flags?

7. Was the experience necessary or could it have been prevented?

Choosing to view your past in this way redirects your mind from the blaming and shaming mindset I described in chapter three, in relation to the learning and growing mindset. Developing the learning and growth mindset is helpful for all situations because it teaches you to be proactive and solution-oriented. It moves you from a victim mentality to a victorious one.

Many people are stuck because they fail to take responsibility for their own life. Don't live like this. Empower yourself by taking ownership of your life and giving yourself permission to move beyond your past.

## Face Your Fears

At the heart of our lack of self-love is fear. I believe most of us fail to enforce the standards we say we have, because we're afraid that the people we want in our lives won't honor them. I've lived my whole life based on fear and let me tell you, it's miserable. You'll either choose to walk by faith and believe that God has the best for you, or you'll continue to settle for less and be unhappy.

Learning how to overcome things that hold you back is how you grow. Confronting your fears is the only way to be free of them (Wow! I think I just set myself free. Lol).

What would that look like? How would it feel to enforce your standards only to have the people you care about decide that they're too high and leave your life? Sit there and feel that for a moment. It's okay to feel. It's okay to be disappointed. It's okay for someone to not want to be a part of your life. We must stop living our lives running from emotional pain and rejection, and with fear of losing people and relationships that will hurt us more in the end.   If someone decides that our bar is too high, that's okay, don't lower them. Do you really want a relationship like that anyway? Is that the kind of relationship you dreamed of as a little girl? I think not!

The fact is that as long as we are here on this earth, people will enter and leave our lives. People we thought would be with us "to the bitter end", as a friend of mine used to say, betray us, or for one reason or another end up leaving our lives. Yes, I know it hurts, but did you die though? (Seriously). We can be so dramatic sometimes thinking we can't live without people, but let me tell you, the only one you don't want to live without is God. The bible says he heals the brokenhearted and binds up their wounds.

He says that he will never leave us or forsake us. He said that even if our mother and father forsake us, he would lift us up. Now tell me you don't need love like that. You don't have to be broken. You don't have to be lonely. You don't have to be miserable. God is ever present and he's given us the strength to overcome our fears.

## Birthing Boundaries

What is it that you want to attract: Your dream job, good friends, maybe a life-long love? Well, what are you doing right now to prepare yourself for what you say that you want? You didn't think it was just going to fall on your lap did you? One of my goals is to attract positive, genuine, trustworthy people into my life who I can build lifelong relationships with.

In order to have these kinds of people in my life, I have to set up boundaries to keep the wrong ones out. When you know what you want, then you know what you are unwilling to accept. It's so important to know yourselves, ladies.

Be leery of anyone who is uncomfortable with you exercising your independence. This is a setup for an abusive relationship.

Healthy people who care about you will have no desire to control you, because they understand that people flourish in freedom. It takes a wise and mature person to think like this, and this is the type of person you want in your life.

A boundary is like a door. Boundaries block the people you don't want and give access to the people you do want in your life. Take the time to write down what you want from a relationship.

What boundaries do you have in place to ensure you get what you are asking? Let's say you want a man who is faithful and trustworthy. Mutual boundaries could be: No flirting with others, and transparency in your relationship. Boundaries can't be one-sided. Relationships are meant to be mutual. Mutuality demonstrates respect. If someone expects something of you that they are unwilling to give, then they don't respect you. The late Aretha Franklin was correct in demanding R-E-S-P-E-C-T, because without it you cannot have real love.

A boundary is not a boundary if it can be broken. You must be so committed to them that you are willing to ride solo if you have to. Many people say that they have boundaries, but when the time comes to enforce them they crumble. Are you willing to compromise who you are for the company of other people? I don't like being around people who smoke. I'm very sensitive to the smell and I feel like I'm suffocating.

So one of my unwritten rules was to never be with people or places where smoke is present. When I was a teen, I met a boy who I really liked. He was one of my brother's friends.

We started spending time together and eventually started dating. We dated on and off for about four years before we called it quits.   I saw him smoking after that, which I thought was odd since I had known him for years and had never seen him smoke. He revealed to me that in one of our first conversations I told him that I didn't like guys who smoke, so he immediately stopped.

People who want to be in your life will happily rise to your level if they really value you. The key word is value. Ladies, some of us have never given any man a chance to value us, because we gave up everything too soon and didn't require anything from them. What makes something valuable is its price, how rare it is, or how much someone wants it.

If a teenage boy can respect a boundary I had when I was fifteen, so can the men or other people who "say" they want to be in your life. Be willing to ride solo if someone is unwilling to raise his bar to meet you on your level.

*Chapter 5 Review*

**Point #1:**

Boundaries are vital because they keep unwanted guests out, and let the ones you do want in. Lowering your standards is counterproductive and will only lead to regret.

**Point #2:**

You're not asking for too much, you're just asking for it from the wrong people. The people who value you will gladly give you what you need without it feeling like a struggle.

**Point #3:**

Having no boundaries is dangerous and will set you up for abuse and mistreatment. People value things that cost them something. A man must be willing to do the work to get you and keep you.

**Point #4:**

You will have to face the fear of rejection if you want to have healthy relationships. God's love is the only love we can't live without. You must learn to be happy in your own company, because there's no guarantee that the relationships you want will always be there. You must learn to be okay with people coming and going from your life; the right ones will stay.

# Girl, Go Get Your Healing

## 6

*If you don't learn how to love yourself first, you'll go from one relationship to the next, without ever giving yourself permission to heal.*

Dealing with toxic people takes a lot of energy. Recovering from someone who is toxic can take months and sometimes even years. We've discussed toxic relationships with others, but what do you do when you have a toxic relationship with yourself? On this journey of life, we should be our greatest ally, but sadly, this isn't always the case.

Growing up in a broken home, developing a broken identity, and being in broken relationships break us. The same way a baby who lacks the nutrients it needs has its growth stunted, we too become stunted in our ability to make rational choices regarding love and relationships, which in turn affects our ability to like ourselves.

We begin to see our mistakes as a reflection of who we are instead of the bad choices we made.

Most people aren't friends with those they don't like. When you don't like yourself, you'll participate in self-sabotaging behaviors, using things like relationships, people-pleasing, and material possessions as a cover-up. In the end, none of these things will bring you the joy and acceptance you desire. You must learn to forgive yourself, value yourself, and love yourself, because you were created for love. Again, once you accept that you were created and are loved by God, it will be easier for you to love and value yourself. He says this about you:

*The LORD your God wins victory after victory and is always with you. He celebrates and sings because of you, and he will refresh your life with his love.*
***-Zephaniah 3:17 (CEV)***

# Pieces of Me

## Part VI

I loved my job and I hated that I had to quit, but I was so terrified. I just wanted to hide and never be found. I had just gotten off work that evening. I was so happy and filled with joy. It was also our one year wedding anniversary. I was excited when I saw our family car in the recovery home driveway when I got home that night. Things were going well, so I thought he was there to take me on a date to celebrate; silly me.

I didn't even stop to check in with the ladies like I normally did. I got inside the car without a second thought, and as soon as I saw the look in his eyes I knew that I had made a big mistake.

When I tried to open the car door to get out, he slugged me in the mouth and held my door closed with one hand and drove off with the other.

After speeding off, he drove recklessly through the streets swerving and threatening to drive the car into people's homes and off a cliff. An unexplainable heavenly peace came over me at that moment and I was no longer afraid. I had gotten so close to God and I trusted that he would take care of me. I could tell that it angered him to know that I was no longer afraid of him. I told him to his face that I wasn't scared of him anymore and that I trust God.

The hate he had for me filled his eyes. I knew he didn't want to hear any of it. The "Christian" man I met years earlier was nowhere to be found. I don't think he ever existed at all. It was just an act. No God-fearing person could treat another human being the way this man had treated his family.

The entire time he drove I was perplexed that I hadn't seen any people I could signal for help. It was a cold chilly winter night, so I guess it's not that surprising. I waited for a cop car to pull up behind us at any moment, but none ever came.

When we came to a quiet residential area, I thought I should try to escape because this man had hell in his eyes and I probably wouldn't survive till morning. I screamed hoping someone would hear me. Every time I reached for the door he would grab it and hold it closed. I tried to pry his big muffin hands from the door but his 6' 1", 300lb frame was too strong for me. No one heard me.

His merciless threats continued and I was exhausted. He drove from one neighborhood to the next, swerving back and forth. Finally, he lost control of the vehicle and crashed my side of the car into a brick wall. How convenient. I was in shock. I had just been in a wreck and adrenaline was blazing through my veins. After the crash, we both exited the car unharmed, by the grace of God. We were alone on the street, the car smoking.

He looked at me with pity in his eyes and said that he was scared and didn't want to lose me. Well, you sure have a sick way of showing it, I thought to myself. For a split-second, I almost felt sorry for him.

I looked at him one last time knowing that if I stayed I would probably be dead the next time. I took off running and didn't look back. I eventually found my way back to the recovery home.

When I got there I told the house manager what had happened. She told me that I should call the police. I was hesitant at first, but I finally got the guts and called. They came over, made a report, and took me to his house to get the kids. He was arrested.

The court put a two year no-contact order in place, and I eventually filed for legal separation. I thought God would punish me for getting a divorce. Thankfully, my ex requested it be turned into a divorce and after much drama, slander, and false accusations, I was a free woman. I don't have time to recount everything that man put me and my children through. All I know is that I'm free, and I thank God that I'm finally free!

Whew chile! I went through so much with that fool. Looking back, I see the signs more clearly. I wish I could go back and change things, but that's not how it all works. When I first escaped, I blamed myself a lot. How did I let this happen? Why this and why that? I have come to understand that people who abuse others are very intentional and crafty. They know exactly what they're doing and they plan it from the start.

Abusers get away with their abuse by blaming their victims and making them think the abuse is their fault.

If you are being abused or are seeing red flags in your relationship, please run as fast as you can.

Abusers rarely change. You'll just end up hurt or maybe even dead. Please don't stay because of children, finances, or out of fear. Make a plan. Contact an abuse hotline or organization. Get out!

Let me say this again: there is zero to slim chances of an abuser changing. I remember speaking to an advocate who worked with abused women for over 25 years. I asked her how many men she knew who had changed during that time. Out of the thousands of women she had counseled, she had only one report of an abusive partner actually changing his way. I know you think your situation is special. I know you think that you're the one out of three-thousand. You're not and you deserve better!

In retrospect, if I had learned how to love myself first, I would have never given my ex the time of day. Remember that day in Denny's when he told me that "God" told him I was his wife? Well, if I can rewrite my story, the conversation would be this way:

**Him:** Yeah! God told me you're my wife. I've been praying for you.

**Me:** Naw n---a, I don't even know you (Eye roll). That sounds like some serial killer ish to me. I don't even like you. Your wife is out there somewhere because it sure ain't me.

Now I'm gonna get up out of this seat and if you try and follow me or contact me again I will get a restraining order! Now thank you for the meal. I bid you good day, sir. (Boom! Mic drop)

*If you don't learn to love yourself first, your desperation will cause you to invite people into your life who were never meant to be a part of it.*

# The 3 "A's" of Healing

Healing is a non-negotiable part of learning to love yourself first. And, you can go about finding healing in various ways. Apostle David Davis from The Greater Life Church in Lakewood, Washington says: "You can't be healed, if you don't be real". Surely, honesty is the first step in finding healing. As for me, one of the ways I've found healing is through what I coined, "The Three A's of Healing: Acknowledgment, Acceptance & Advancement.

## Acknowledgment

Something is broken. It's hard to admit this because most of us grew up being strong out of necessity, not something we chose to be. It was a survival instinct. Admitting that there is something inside of you needing repair can make you feel vulnerable. Once I was able to overcome shame and acknowledge that I needed healing, I was able to address the parts of me that needed mending.

I found out that I struggled with the fear of rejection and fear of being abandoned. These fears caused me to become a people pleaser and extremely self-critical. It was easier for me to blame myself, because I could always fix myself.

Admitting that the people I loved had hurt me and were unwilling to take responsibility for it was devastating; but once I learned to place the responsibility back where it belonged, which is the other person, it became empowering. It was freeing to no longer beat myself up for the things that others did to me. With the help of a therapist and a lot of personal work, I was able to move forward.

## Acceptance

After the acknowledgment phase comes the acceptance. In this step you take responsibility for any role, if any, that you played. This isn't about blaming, but about taking back control of your life. It's empowering. As you look back at your experience, was there something you could've done? No, we cannot control the actions of others. If someone wants to hit you, then that's what he's going to do. What you do after the event is what's important. Again, this is not about placing blame, but about empowerment.

If abuse happened when you were a child, please know that it was not your fault. It is not your responsibility to bear the shame of what others have done. In this case you will simply need to accept that other people hurt you, it was wrong, and as a child you were powerless to do anything about it. Give yourself permission to live free from the pain of your past experiences.

Please remember that abuse is never the victim's fault; however, if you are an adult and decide to stay with someone who abuses you, then you are not loving yourself. You are subconsciously approving the other person's behavior by staying in a relationship with them.

This was hard for me to accept at first, but looking back can see how staying in a toxic relationship sent the wrong message. Think about a mother and a child. The child frequently throws tantrums to get what she wants. The mother tells the child that she won't get it if she throws a tantrum, but instead of following through, the mother gives in and gives the child what she wants.

Her example speaks louder than her words, and the child learns that throwing a fit will get her what she wants. This same thing happens in our relationships. We forget that people learn from our actions and not just our words. If words and actions don't line up, they mean nothing.

Additionally, red flags are often seen early on before our hearts get involved. Our intuition may tell us something is off, a family member may say they don't have a good feeling about a person, or maybe the person shows you they have a temper. Whatever the signs and whatever your reason for ignoring them, they will cost you. You can't go back and change what was done to you or the things that you allowed, but you can begin to take your power back through acceptance. This process would look something like this:

**You:** I stayed in a toxic relationship because I thought that he loved me. I didn't know that I was condoning his toxic behavior with my presence, and that was not loving myself.

Now I realize that I should never allow someone to mistreat me, no matter what. People who love me will not intentionally hurt me.

I should've loved myself enough to leave the relationship when I knew that it was no longer good for me. I forgive myself for staying. I forgive myself for allowing others to mistreat me.

From now on, I will do the work of learning how to love and value myself, so that I can teach others how to love and value me too.

## Advancement

The next phase is advancement. This is where you begin to thrive in spite of your experiences. You can allow healing into your life by speaking the truth over the lies that make you believe you're not good enough.

Examples:

**Lie #1:** It's too late for me, I'll never find love.

Truth: I may have made mistakes, but it's never too late. I deserve love. I was created for love. I allow love into my life. It is mine. I will have it.

**Lie #2:** I will always end up in bad relationships. I should stop trying.

Truth: I was created for relationships. Good people are coming into my life to stay. I will never give up on the healthy love and relationships I desire to have. I will work on myself while I'm waiting.

**Lie #3:** I'll never be happy.

Truth: I was meant to enjoy my life and be happy. I will never stop pursuing my own peace and happiness. I have a future and a hope given to me by God.

When you begin to shift your focus from the pain of the past to the promises of the future, your life will start to come together. Take back the pen of your life and write yourself a new story. To get to this point, it may be necessary to get some counseling or see a therapist.

You need a place to release your pain, a safe person to help you make sense of the things you've experienced. I've been to therapy several times in my life and let me tell you, I've never regretted a second of it. Sometimes friends can be well meaning, but you may need a professional to help you see clearly and gain a new perspective.

I also recommend finding a creative outlet for your emotions such as journaling, painting, poetry, music, or dancing. Anything you enjoy doing can be therapeutic and can help relieve stress. In this phase, you realize that the things meant to break you have only made you stronger. Shame has no place in this space. You're doing the work and you're getting better day by day.

## Discovering Your Worth

What makes a person worthy? What makes a person valuable? Are we worthy based upon the way we look? Is our worthiness based upon the things we possess, or our accomplishments? The answer to this question will differ for each person you ask. According to God, you are worthy because you were created and are loved by him. If you let the world tell you that you're not good enough because you're not the right size, color, or you weren't born into the right family, you'll never learn to love yourself.

If your worth is based upon outward appearances, then you are doomed to a life of unhappiness because there will always be someone prettier, smarter, and who has more money than you. You will always find a need to compare yourself to others, and it will never be enough. Just ask all the famous people who have committed suicide over the years.

If money, fame, and beauty were enough, then the people in Hollywood would be the happiest people in the world.

The point I'm trying to make is this: you can't base your worth on temporary things. Believing you are worthy is a choice; it's an act of faith. You don't need anyone to validate it. You don't need another person to agree with you. You only need to stand in agreement with yourself, believing you are worthy of all the good things that life has to offer you.

It doesn't matter if you're twenty pounds overweight or at your weight goal. It's not dependent on you having your dream job or you working at McDonald's. It's that inner confidence of knowing that you bring something undeniably unique and beautiful to this world. Refuse to allow unworthiness to stop you from living the life you deserve.

## Self-Love Everyday

Learning to love yourself first is a lifelong journey. You won't always get it right, but as you continue to learn and grow, you will get better and better at setting boundaries, giving yourself what you need, and asking for what you want. It's really an exciting process when you think about it.

Most have lived their lives waiting for others to give them what they want, like flowers from their secret crush on Valentine's Day, or a special gift from a significant other on their birthday.There's nothing wrong with people doing things for you. The key is not to solely depend on them, because people will eventually disappoint you in one way or another.

When you learn how to be happy, independent of other people, then the sting of disappointment will have little to no effect on you. Self-love is freeing because the only person you need to be happy is you. Everything else is just icing on the cake.

My life has not been easy and I've overcome many challenges, but the most rewarding thing that I've ever done is learn to love myself first. Learning to love yourself takes the pressure off of your relationships and gives you the ability to love others from a place of abundance instead of emptiness. So how do you practice self-love everyday? You take the knowledge, wisdom, and tips you've learned in this book and apply them to your life. These include:

- Creating boundaries for all of your relationships;
- Having standards that you live by;
- Holding others accountable for their actions, including yourself;
- Having mutually beneficial relationships that bring peace and joy to your life;

- Taking care of your mind, body, and spirit by giving it what it needs daily;

- Respecting your need for downtime by not planning too many activities into your day or overextending yourself;

- Letting go of toxic people and relationships, so that you can grow and flourish;

- Allowing yourself to heal by getting counseling;

- Not jumping too quickly into another relationship;

- Engaging in therapeutic activities that you enjoy;

- Believing in yourself enough to invest in yourself, and pursuing your dreams; and

- Continuing to better yourself through reading books, getting a coach, and mentorship.

These are just a few ways you can practice self-care everyday. You are a unique individual, so you will need to tailor these examples to fit your life. You will also need to add things to this list as you change and discover more about yourself. I'm so proud of the work you've done in this book. I know that your life will get better, and you'll become the woman you are meant to be.

Apply these principles and have faith in yourself. Also, don't be too hard on yourself. You're only human.

Lasting change takes time. Don't give up. The world needs you. Never be afraid to shine bright. You'll never know who needs your light.

## Worth the Wait

You are worth waiting for. True love is worth waiting on. Building healthy relationships are worth the effort. Becoming your best self is worth the work that's required to make it come to pass. There are two ways that you can learn in life: One is by making the mistakes yourself; the other is to learn from the mistakes of others.

There are enough people in the world who have already made the mistakes for you, so why waste time? Many people fail to learn from their mistakes because they never stop long enough to evaluate what went wrong and how to prevent it from happening again. Don't be one of those people. Others fail to learn because they are too stubborn, or find it hard to hear from the person trying to help them. I was like that. Don't be like me.

One piece of wisdom I can give you about learning from the mistakes of others is this: *Never let the messenger hinder the message.* There's something that you can learn from every person. Everyone has some type of wisdom that they can share to help others. A drug addict can warn you about the dangers of using recreational drugs.

A teenage mother can encourage young girls to respect themselves and save themselves for marriage. You can learn by making mistakes, or you can learn from heartache. Which one will you choose? Be humble enough to listen and wise enough to know when God is trying to teach you. Take what you need and leave what you don't.

I know that waiting can be hard because you feel like you're missing out on something. Sometimes the only thing you're missing out on is the pain that God is trying to save you from. There's a time for everything. If you have to wait longer than you think you should, it is for a reason and you must trust God. Don't try to make things happen on your own.

You are worth the wait. Real love and healthy relationships are worth waiting on. Work on yourself, build your dreams, and create the life you've always dreamed of. Become the woman that you've always wanted to be. With God, nothing is impossible. I believe in you. God believes in you. Take a look in the mirror and start believing in yourself. The world is waiting for you too. Love Yourself First!

*Chapter 6 Review*

**Point #1:**

The 3 "A's" of Healing are: Acknowledgment, Acceptance, and Advancement. You must be willing to face your pain, accept any responsibility you have, and advance by moving toward your future with faith and hope. Healing is an essential part of your journey. Give yourself the space and tools you need to heal, so you can be your best self.

**Point #2:**

You must begin to see yourself as worthy. You were created by God and He loves you. God's love is what gives you worth and value. His love can never be taken away. It is eternal. Understanding and accepting God's love for your life will make it easier for you to love yourself.

**Point #3:**

Self-love is not a one-time act, but something you must practice and perfect on a daily basis. Daily self-love is easy to practice once you begin to believe in your own worth. You won't be perfect, but never give up on loving, learning, and growing into the woman you want to be.

**Point #4:**

Love is worth the wait. Don't be in a hurry to jump into relationships. Learn from your own mistakes and the mistakes of others. Work on yourself while you wait. You were created for good things and they will find you at the right time.

# Self-Love Affirmations

When you learn how to love yourself first, you'll find a new world of opportunity begin to open up for you. The affirmations written below are powerful tools to use on your self-love journey. Speak these life-giving words over yourself daily, memorize them, write them down, and develop your own. I am so proud of the work you've done and the woman you are becoming. Remember to be patient with yourself, and never forget that you are not alone. You deserve the best!

I am enough.

I am whole.

I am healed.

I have peace.

I am worthy of love.

I lack no good things.

I have everything I need to be happy.

I forgive myself for all my past mistakes.

I forgive myself for allowing others to mistreat me.

I forgive myself for mistreating myself.

I will be honest with myself, even when it hurts.

I accept myself just as I am.

What I want and need is important.

My body is beautiful.

My mind is brilliant.

Everyday I am taking steps to improve myself.

I am focused & motivated.

I am surrounded by blessings.

I am kind & generous.

I have lots to offer.

I have something to smile about.

I deserve nothing but the best.

I am an amazing woman.

I am fearless.

I am strong and confident.

I will accomplish all my goals & dreams.

I will not be afraid of failure.

I will never give up.

I will never stop trying.

I will not be afraid to ask for the help I need.

I willingly receive God's blessings.

I will partner with people of purpose.

My life matters.

God has good things in store for me.

My future is bright.

I have what it takes to make it & look good while doing it.

I will be genuine and authentic.

I have unlimited potential.

The only thing that can stop me is me.

# The 10 "I's" of Self-Love

You are worthy and deserving of love. Use these statements daily to remind yourself of your worth and value. Write them down somewhere you can see them. Remember, there is power in your words. Don't be afraid to use them!

### 1.

I will love myself first, because I can't pour from an empty cup. It's the only way I can love God and others.

### 2.

I will hold others accountable for their actions without guilt or fear of rejection, because those who deserve to be in my life will treat me right.

### 3.

I will allow people into my circle who have proven they deserve to be there, because who I allow into my life will affect it for better or worse.

### 4.

I will be patient with myself and forgive myself for any mistakes I've made, because unforgiveness hinders creativity and my ability to grow.

### 5.

I take responsibility for my own life and I will not make excuses for myself or others, because the only person I am responsible for is me.

### 6.

I will never stop pursuing self-improvement, growth, and healing, because in order to be happy I must be whole.

### 7.

I will not allow toxic thoughts, people, or environments to control me, because I choose to thrive and live a positive life.

### 8.

I will not allow disappointments or setbacks to throw me off course, because I have a purpose, and every roadblock is just another stepping stone to my success.

**9.**

I give myself permission to be the person God created me to be without fearing rejection from others, because the world doesn't need another counterfeit. It needs me. I need me!

**10.**

I will find something about myself to celebrate daily, because I must be my biggest fan and greatest encouragement.

*God is within her, she will not fall; God will help her at break of day.*
***-Psalms 46:5***

*Hello Today*

Yesterday I was abused, but today I refuse; hello today.

Yesterday I survived, but today I'm gonna thrive; hello today.

Yesterday I fell, but today I'm gonna rise; hello today.

Yesterday I felt like nothing, but today I know I'm something; hello today.

Yesterday I was broken, but today I know God's still working; hello today.

Yesterday I was hurt, because I didn't know my worth; hello today.

Yesterday I cried, but I didn't die; hello today.

Yesterday is gone, it hurt like hell, but I'm still standing

strong; hello today.

Sometimes I dread you, wishing I could just go back to bed

too; hello today.

I know they say everyday that your mercies are new,

but sometimes I struggle to believe in you.

Yeah, I said it... sometimes I still struggle to believe in

YOU! Hello today!

Life is hard! It comes with good and lots of bad, but today I

choose joy over just feeling sad;

hello today.

I choose not to be defeated, I pick myself up off the

ground, sweaty hands, bruised and bleeding.

Now I know we haven't always been best friends,

but I'm gonna celebrate, because this is not how my story

ends; hello today.

You see, I refuse to give up on you.

I will put on wisdom before I rise up to meet you;

hello today.

Now I know today, that you'll never be perfect,

but I just wanted to say,

Today! ... You're still WORTH IT!

# Resource List

**Phone Numbers:**

The National Domestic Violence Hotline

1-800-799-SAFE (7233)

**Websites:**

joinonelove.org

loveisrespect.org

thehotline.org

**Suggested Books:**

1. **Self-Love Everyday**: 31 Empowering Affirmations by Krystle Laughter

2. **Queenology** by R.C. Blakes

3. **Let's Be Honest**: Real Answers for Real Women Facing Abuse by Krystle Laughter

4. **A Woman's Influence** by Tony & Sheri Gaskins

5. **The Father Daughter Talk** by R.C. Blakes

6. **Unholy Charade**: Unmasking the Domestic Abuser in the Church by Jeff Crippen & Rebecca Davis

7. **Why Does He Do That**: Inside the Minds of Angry & Controlling Men by Lundy Bancroft

8. **Make it Work** by Tony Gaskins

9. **Keeping the Faith**: Guidance for Christian Women Facing Abuse by Marie M. Fortune

10. **The After Abuse Series** *(Fall 2020)* by Krystle Laughter

**Music:**

All Things New by Krystle Laughter-Parker

# About the Author

***Krystle Laughter*** is an author, certified life coach, writer, recording artist & mother of seven. She began writing as a youth and enjoys creating poetry, spoken-word, and music.

She has a passion for inspiring others and utilizes her online platforms to empower women through self-love and personal development.

Krystle is a true overcomer and overachiever who has triumphed to become the woman she is today. If you need help achieving your goals, accountability, motivation, or healing from the past, book her as your life coach today.

Krystle also helps aspiring authors through author consulting. She can provide manuscript feedback, create a unique book cover, as well as develop a beautiful layout for your nonfiction book. Email her at ***krystlelaughter@gmail.com*** to learn more.

Follow her on YouTube, Instagram, Facebook & Twitter **@krystlelaughter** for more inspiration.

# MUSIC

# All Things New

Krystle released her debut album, *All Things New* in 2014.
Songs like *Black is Beautiful, Hollow & New Life* speak to
the struggles of women and the power to overcome. *All
Things New* will keep you bobbing your head to uplifting
tracks like: *Sparkle & Highway to the Sky,* while songs
like: *He Made You Beautiful* will leave you feeling
empowered. Stream it online today!

BOOKS

*Now Available*

# SELF-LOVE
*Everyday*

31 Empowering Affirmations

KRYSTLE LAUGHTER

AUTHOR OF LOVE YOURSELF FIRST

# Let's Be Honest

REAL ANSWERS

FOR REAL WOMEN

FACING ABUSE

KRYSTLE
LAUGHTER

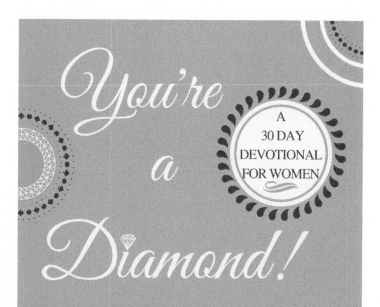

*You're*

*a*

*Diamond!*

A
30 DAY
DEVOTIONAL
FOR WOMEN

UNCOVER
THE
DIAMOND IN
YOU!

Fearfully

&

Wonderfully

Made

-Psalm 139:114

Krystle Laughter

*When I Think of You* is the perfect gift for children and
adults alike; it provides a sweet way to honor the memory
of a lost loved one by meditating on the good times. Share
the joy now in...*When I Think of You.*

International Selling Author

Supports Early Childhood Education

# Anna's Dancing Animal Alphabet

Krystle Laughter

# AFTER **ABUSE** SERIES

## *Coming Fall 2020*

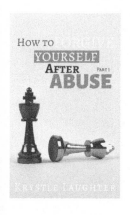

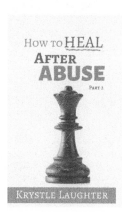

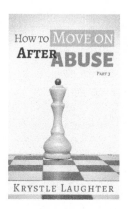

## COMING 2021

# love Yourself again.

How to Set Standards, Create Healthy
Boundaries & Stop Being a Doormat

*International Selling Author*

# KRYSTLE LAUGHTER

Made in the USA
Las Vegas, NV
17 June 2021

24922764R00100